洞月亮

CAVE MOON PRESS
YAKIMA中WASHINGTON

2019

The Making

Gerry McFarland

洞月亮

CAVE MOON PRESS

YAKIMA 中 WASHINGTON

ISBN: 978-0-9797785-1-3

The Making

For Shield

[signature]

Thanks for
the interview!

Acknowledgements

"Rejected by a Little Magazine, the Poet Repairs the Faucet," *Zyzzyva, Wisconsin Review*
"I Heard the Word Ohio," *Bellowing Ark*
"Allegra's Garden," *Berkeley Poetry Review*
"The Making," *Crucible*
"Camano Island by Car," *Crab Creek Review*
"Skipping Stones," *Bayou, Sanskrit*
"Snapshot at the Border," *Bayou*
"Coming to Light," *RiverSedge*
"When Rick Died, Linda Said," *Limestone*
"Crossing Agate Pass Bridge At Night," *South Dakota Review*
"Four Poems," *Convolvulus*
"Starlight Dome Car," *Detours: Poems Of Travel By Land, Air, Sea And Mind*
"The Oak and the Grave," *Phi Kappa Phi Forum*
"Looking Out My Window, Three AM, In Fremont," *4 AM*
"My Father's Scar," "Monsoon," *Talking River*
"Angiogram," *Soundings East*
"Asthma," *Cider Press Review*
"Code Blue," *Gemini Magazine*
"Gunner's Go-Go Girl Dream," *Contemporary American Voices*

POEMS

I

II

III

Whatsoever thy hand findeth to do, do it with thy might, for there is neither wisdom nor glory in the grave.

Ecclesiastes 9:10

I

Monsoon

for Joyce

I want to tell you about the monsoon
The plank bridge from the gate
Of Subic Bay Naval Station
To Olongapo, over the yellow river
Children dived in for coins,

How the monsoon made Olongapo
A lake, men into dark silhouettes
Slow as divers on the dirt town's
Nameless single road and held
This white-clad sailor, American

Dollars hidden in damp shoes,
Pink and blue fringed canopies
Of jeepnees lurched and splashed
The puddled road past monkey meat
On fire drum spits, the fountain ringed

By stone faces chipped in every
Election's gunfire, baby ducks
Thrown to alligators for a peso.
In the monsoon's spontaneous
Embrace, I thought of you in that clean

And sunny yard while the monsoon
Baptized Olongapo, granted
Extravagant forgiveness, made
The road dark slop, tin rooftops
Rattle, then stopped. That was the last

Time I saw Olongapo, my uniform
Translucent in the warm flood,
The brown bottle of San Miguel
I drank outside in the mud, long
Before Mt. Pinotubo plumed

Over Mindanao, Luzon,
And thick gray dust grew
To wind-blown shapes of pickup trucks
On the abandoned base, and Olongapo
Strangled in soft, hot feathers.

Never saw the Philippines
Beyond Olongapo. Never saw
The rain tree forest, the swing of light
In another country. Olongapo,
Olongapo, Olongapo,

Once full of sticks and gunfire,
Deepened in a new volcanic skin,
Jeepnees axles wound
With the tendrils of the koa,
I enter your dark street
with a shovel and an axe.

The Making

for Tim

Closed on a hammer his hands
Are like hills,
Swollen places
On the earth;
Palms open,
Become
Rough plains, each line

A minute stream bed circling
Discolored
Calluses. At evening
Seated
Under kitchen light, elbows
On his knees palms open

As a stubble field,
He picks at scabs,
Fingers newly blistered faults
In a ritual of reparation
To the God of the Unfinished.

Tomorrow his hands will make a house.
Mute instruments
Will build from air
The fact of wood,
Join opposing forests. There must be

A new word for such making.
In morning light, on the hill,
Pine studs will frame the house
Of the new word,
The molten sun

Light the house's bones.
The hands
Will start things off.
Blocks will hold promise
And the smells of pine,
Sawdust, earth, and rain will be new.

Rejected by a Little Magazine, the Poet Repairs the Faucet

In the window of our cramped yellow kitchen
Light fractures in the cherry branches.
The blossoms fell last month
Pink edits on the fresh green page.

Deep in the faucet the gasket is worn.
Water sputters in the silver throat
And the whole thing bangs and quakes.
Light steps in the leaves of the cherry,

Fixes me to the floor, wrench in one hand,
Lead neck of the battered fixture
In the other. Damp dark stuff
Sent up unfiltered into every kitchen

Drips black onto the floor, pools
On linoleum, a tiny black lake
Of corroded iron. Once I ran
A plumbers' snake down under the kitchen sink,

Down the larynx of our house,
Into the bowels until it gurgled, popped,
And spit back loose crap from the deep.
But this is a simple repair. Just a humble

Little pink washer. There. One branch
In the window frame jerks like an elbow
Deleting thoughts, ending sentences.
White fists of light cross the room.

Fly back into the cherry tree
Apart from the plumbed world
To mingle with leaves, shake loose
The last of the soft pink thumb prints.

Skipping Stones, San Fernando Valley, 1964

I remember the sway of her forearm gentle
As she stepped small by my side up the hill
To the dam at the end of the steep boulevard.

The man-made lake. Summers then were loose,
Sunny, long as the warm sidewalk uphill
From her yellow house. We didn't know the dam

Would burst when the fingers of the old fault
Worked loose the bound water onto
The evacuated neighborhood. We were

Thirteen. We didn't know she would be thrown
From a horse in Denver, restrained in the brilliant room
While they set the bone, scrubbed the wounds.

We knew the words to Unchained Melody
And all the names of the Beach Boys. We were the small
Flesh of the world. We didn't know the imminence

Of her father's death. I didn't know
What it meant when my forearm brushed against hers.
The stone has to look like this, I told her.

She showed a girl's disinterest, wandered, mute
Down the shore, touching the hair she had spent
The last hour setting. I demonstrated

How to fit the stone in the knuckle, bend close
To the water, swing the arm parallel the earth.
I threw my heart out the end of my fingers.

My Father's Scar

Doctors said the flesh would grow back
But it never did. As children,
My brother and I were not to speak of it.
I imagined Geronimo

Had scalped the white man in his sleep.
When I was eleven I lifted my shirt
On the schoolyard to show the scar from
My appendectomy. I had something

Missing too, another secret that
Wasn't. Endless sunlight fell
On the yellow house among the shadows
Of orange groves. Rows of silver quonset

Huts of migrant workers shimmered.
I learned a word: "developer."
Huge machines ripped up the groves
And left the pulpy trunks like green

Soldiers parallel the ground,
The dark roots like hands crusted
With the soil of their graves
reached toward us as we ran by,

Rotting oranges in our fists
For the long food-fight summer.
A kid I knew—Steve—was killed
When he flew on a bike out from between

Parked cars. The word—Steve—
Became his sister's face. What
She said afterward. Then the
Trees were gone and the huge,

Dust-flying field grew whole streets
That lined themselves with two-
Story houses. My brother joined
The Army. I drove a red Chevy

Convertible to the beach on school
Days, ate frozen bananas,
My toes in the friendly tide
While dutiful students attended primly

In their seats and scribbled notes.
I acted on my own desire.
My parents watched Vietnam
And *Gunsmoke* on television.

I was the last kid in the house,
The not-my-brother. I thought of myself
As the wind, where my car went.
But deep in the silence, I knew

The not-my-brother was a scar,
Torn from the earth like the long dead
Groves, in a car the color of blood,
A red slash on the road.

Family Snapshot

He leaned on the Chrysler's enormous, bulbous fender,
Planted me, the youngest, on his knee, stood my brother
In front like a sentry, scooped our sister up with one arm
And crushed the skirt of her frilly white summer dress.

He held her so that her shoulder twisted. She smiled
Beautifully like she always did. The bow in her hair skewed
Against his starched white shirt. She smiled beautifully
Like she always did. The car shined. The neighborhood

Spread out behind us like a panorama, like some pristine,
Long-desired ranch, a Hollywood empire with manicured
Lawns, big front doors, and long driveways to the paved future.
Nothing could ever go wrong again. Under the forgiving

Sunlight of Los Angeles, we had everything. We all smiled.
My sister smiled beautifully as she always did. She and I
Looked at this old shot and reminisced about slow shutter speeds.
The black hair on the back of his hand blurred in the froth of her dress.

My Sister's Face

My sister's face is pale as the white sand
On a beach in California, so soft
That when touched the structure of bone
Beneath it surprises; one expects
The fingers to sink in, her flesh to melt,

Subside, a changing landscape in the hand.
She and I, young in the San Fernando Valley,
In the little identical towns crushed
Between the smoking, crawling city, Los Angeles,
And the huge round empty dusty hills.

On television, a man demonstrated to beginners
How to draw a face: first, a loose circle,
Oblong, though. Just practice that. Now a line
Through the center of that circle and two smaller
Circles, like holes in a plate, for the eyes.

My sister's face is like an unfinished drawing.
Her eyes plain and light, though I want
Them dark, penetrating. The tiny creases could be
From years of squinting in hard sunlight.
She may wince at a harsh remark. A little skin

May gather at the eyes when her mouth
Takes the shape of a question and she begins
As softly as the little gyres of wind
In the baked, vacant school yards,
The red in her short brown hair unclear

Until the sun, diffusing, makes a color
Which can't be sustained, gold, at my sister's temple.

Scoutmaster

Never lost driving any suburb in LA,
He gripped himself like a steering wheel.

He looked straight ahead all the time.
He could drive anywhere in a straight line.

Every time he turned the wheel, the world
Straightened out. Each new house meant more

Than what had been left, sold, unsaid.
He just kept his hands on the wheel.

Sometimes when he looked into the mirror
I thought he was trying to see backward

As if to find that one thing fallen from the truck
He'd not been quick enough to save.

He took my brother and me, his two sons,
Fishing once at a man-made lake

Where you paid to fish a stock of trout
With rented bamboo poles, strings tied to the ends.

I remember his thick fingers fooling
With the string and the tiny knot, trying

To see into it, untangle it. He drove us back,
Arm straight out, wrist hooked on the wheel

Of the black truck, eye on the mirror, as if to see
A dozen trout in the bed come back to life.

Asthma

1954

Following the doctor's orders, we moved
Farther from Los Angeles—escaped
The dingy smoke over the harbor, the yellow
Callouses of smog, the black waste

On the gray horizon like bombs that plumed
And stained the windows, darkening the houses
Fifty miles away—but hadn't moved
Far enough. The trees panicked, put out

Their arms against the window, assaulted darkness
While the illness climbed the sill. Death
To me was a story I had always wanted
To hear, a question to be answered. I asked again.

No, she whispered. *No*. She cradled me,
And rocked us both; her heart beat in my ear.

The Greatest Generation

San Fernando Valley, 1944

Two little boys, barefoot and shirtless
Ribs like wings, fight with wooden swords

In a grassy yard. Their mother leans
On one elbow in the peaceful grass.

She thinks that she should stop them
But they are laughing, and their father

Would say to let them be. He is learning,
He wrote in his last letter, to speak

Italian. The boys' happiness
Echoes like the phonograph

At night in the empty living room.
The younger runs to his mother,

Crying out, a splinter in his finger.
She puts an end to the little war.

The Viewing

You look like stone.
Your crisp dress
Is peculiar,

Hands gray
And
Cold as a valley

Stream descendant
From the glacier,
Your face sealed

Against the flood.
I regret
Thinking of you

As stone, but you
Are not yourself—
I want you to begin

In the middle
Of a thought,
As you often did,

As if startled,
Interrupted,
But you don't

And this surprises me
Twice: once
Because you are silent

Twice because
I did not, somehow,
Expect silence.

Your death
Occurs to me then:
The one end-stopped

Thought, a space
To calculate
The distance to

The cemetery
Alone
With what remains.

An Old Handwritten Letter from My Mother

I'd torn it.
Thought:
Throw it out
Like an old

Casserole
After a family
Potluck, so
Ordinary,

Familial
As heart disease—
A niece pregnant
Out of wedlock,

The conditions
Of a loan—
But the paper, blue-lined
And thick, smells

Like an old school desk
The kind with a hole
For a bottle of ink.
The G in my name

Sweeps up the way
She fixed her hair
In a cursive
No longer taught

In public schools.
The post office
Is bankrupt. But this
Is her accounting:

The scratch of the pen
Lettering,
Orderly
As the quiet trees.

Allegra's Garden

The street is filled with plants and vines.
Morning glory thread the rims
Of my neighbor's car. He takes pruning
Shears to the arms and hands to free

Them from the frame, axles, tires,
Steer the old Chrysler into
Dirt until it too grows branches,
And little chrome bulbs fall to the ground.

Clematis overtook the house,
A mass of white blooms in a tangle
Of green and brown branches threaded
Like folded arms. Hydrangeas wave

At passersby who wave back,
Speechless, step and dodge through daisies
Wide as dinner plates, stems
Thick as trees. Rose branches crack

Concrete. We feast on tree root steak,
Begonia salad. Everything
Grows back. The arm of the cherry tree,
Long since reached the kitchen window,

Befriended the rafters. We eat its blossoms.
Sunflowers see the vegetables
Fall unharmed from raised beds.
Tree roots broken through the floor

Become chairs, western hemlock
A table. We gave up trying to leave.
Worried once about all this growing,
Our limbs turning an earthy hue,

Hair thick and green, our faces
Round as sunflowers. We speak the language
Of growing things, the ubiquitous
Zucchini, our giant heads nodding.

Doxology In Four Parts

1

Hymns rose out of oak and stone,
We thought, to save us. The pastor's raiments
Swung as he bowed to every kneeling supplicant:
This is my body. Take and eat. This is my blood.

The choir, faces lifted, praised the sacrament.
A pretty ritual for you and me. A trinity of you
Me and it. A cerebral dance, something to wear.
We stopped our ceremony with the wine.

Our Remembrance was blacked out.
Convulsed with laughter and vomit
We never nailed our theses to the door.
Never really believed.

2

Our vision was apotheosis
In a shaky duplex. Giggling,
Squat on the floor watching flies
Dive-bomb in an empty room.

Broadway was alive with sadness
In the smiling gay men. God
Guided us politely to the ferry.
We followed, apostolic, chaste

Across illuminated water
To Winslow and its golden promise,
Faced the wind, sensed the Luminosity—
A couple of Lutherans.

3

Once more we tried donuts
On Fourth Avenue. Once more
I observed what endures: one corner
Of your mouth lower than the other;

When you chewed or spoke
It pulled inward then down, circular,
Natural as a birth defect. Grinning,
Mouth full of dough, you touched the paper napkin

To the powdered sugar clinging to your cheek.
We were finished. You stepped from the curb
Into traffic stopped for you, glanced back once
And said: "Goodbye, ex-husband."

4

We haven't spoken since. Our child,
A miscarriage, would have been twelve.
The receiver is wrong in my hand.
Forgive these

Punctuating silences, but this is how
We talk now. Outside my window
Acquaintances in a passing car mouth
Something spoken but unheard

From open faces. We never spoke of it.
What language silence has become.
We exchange our words as carefully as rings.
But I have fallen in love with silence.

Self Portrait

Hard to see truly at a glance.
A rock pock-marked in the acne era,
Worn in the reckless age by drunken wind,
The dark forest at the clearing's edge.

Like looking down at land from a plane.
The alpine face. Note the graying border.
The eyes fold deeply brown
Into fleshy lids, make little valleys,

Crease the hills of the bony sockets.
I hope to find in the glass what will make
It sensible. Everything. Cheeks cut
Like stream beds down from eyes,

The bone of the impermanent skull.
The eyes have it. The eyes design the seen.
Here is the self, divided in bifocals,
A body under incandescent heavens.

The Mirror

The face in the bathroom mirror could be me.
I always tried to count the beers I drank.

Pool stick in hand, I lifted high the bottle
And announced: *Gentlemen, this is number three.*

Always, I then lost count. The coffee tastes like pepper.
Atop the neck my head lolls like a stone.

My sleeve is damp from dragging it across my open mouth.
The globes of my eyes fracture into little red rivers.

My skin is dead. My hands rocks. The water
from the faucet pointed as steel knives,

I shove my hands into it and stab my face until it bleeds.

Camano Island by Car

for Rick and Linda

When we drove the long hills
Adrift in the eye of a storm of color
And the land rose and fell green,
How did we keep our senses,

Keep locked our stumbling features,
Not fall from the open sedan
Foolish to the sweet earth
Drunk with beauty?

Two red lines on the map meant,
With faith, we would find our place:
The intersecting fence-posts,
The broad porch on the hill.

In the dappled yard, by the arbor
Stooped over a new beech
They looked up, shouted.
Each waved one free arm.

Gunner's Go-Go Girl Dream

She turns on the bar top,
face lifted to strobe-lit heaven,
eyes closed, the little hills

of her ankles fluid as the surf,
the mounds of her hips
twin atolls that narrow

to the peninsula of her bare
waist under spare dim
moons, soulful, human

in a long dark world
of spilled beer and glitter.
Her moon face up in lights

an island, tropical
as sand. Does she, her face
like a moon over the ocean,

desire? My heart is at sea,
rudder shifting port
to starboard, rising and falling

in a vast body. The stars
of her own island planet
blink. She dances on,

the bar top long as a dock,
a harbor break in the darkness,
and we, her suppliants

like little gigs at the toes
of her pointed shoes bob
in her wind. The door to the bar

opens onto Broadway,
San Diego. Horns
crash, engines throttle,

headlamps and streetlights
reveal the bouncer, bored,
sober, slumped on his stool,

checking IDs with a flashlight.
I could leave, unmoor
from this dock, but the beer

is cold and all there is
on the street are the hawks
selling gilt-edged bibles.

Here the light softens
on her skin, her hips
drift in the rhythmic tide,

and her long, dark, curled
hair falls on the swells
of her breasts and gleams

like the moon and stars
on a black sea on a clear night.
In one turn she is dancing

In front of me. She looks
down at me from the glory
of her painted face,

into my adoration,
and dawns into a smile
meant for me alone

and I dream the two of us
in a red Stingray top down
driving to Tijuana,

her fingers in my hair,
a gust of wind from the road,
tires rolling like the ocean.

Riverhouse

Greenville, New Hampshire

For Wren

The river crashes over stacks of rock.
On waking, I thought it was traffic noise
An air conditioner perhaps, not
The river, placid little Greenville poised
On either bank. I had forgotten where
I was in the dawn whispering late out
Of darkness—not in the clatter or steel air
Of cities but in the unhurried place about
The river, enduring syllable of longing
From the mountains, above which trees uncross
And cross against the sky. The river's song
Is deep and full as my sleep had been, now lost.
So far, my waking slow has understood
A river in the dark. I'd stay if I could.

Coming To Light

for Allegra

That I could meet what comes as easily—
Fix the back screen door, clean the gutters,
Plug the leak, replace the washer, see
That the rattling faucet in the kitchen sputters
Less—as the first of the morning lights upon
The room, illuminates the spackled ceiling,
Spills into the murky hallway on
To many nameless jobs to be done. This cleaning
Light, dust-filled, finds you still asleep,
Dawns on us in our disheveled house.
It's time to come. And you, my wife, deep
In your dream of a brighter, more useful kitchen, rouse.
In the beginning, speechless, we embrace.
We start out in this unfinished place.

Squall

A muddy stream of coffee in the sink
Splashes in the raining faucet, a little storm
In the kitchen. Outside, the squall gathers.
Stratus shoulders in like men in gray

Flannel muttering in the blue room.
Rain's indecipherable syllables
Gather in cupped pavement, glisten
On passing cars, patter where the tree root's

Elbow broke through asphalt in the street
In front of the house, a swollen river
Oil-streaked from countless crankcases,
Eddies to a lake slashed with rain

At the deepest intersection. A page hangs
In the storm drain, ink bleached from its thesis
And drenched branches wave like the arms
Of the drowning, hands open as leaves.

North Bound

First Avenue
South, moves

My blue car
The city swallows

Into its lights.
The viaduct,

Queen Anne,
The arc of the highest

Bridge, Aurora,
A string of moons

Across a canal.
What happens is light.

Light at the shipping
Lanes leaves

No shadows
Over acres

Of stacked yellow
And orange containers.

Cranes like giant
Herons. The ferry

A circle of light
bound for the

Peninsula
And its braid of light.

Light spills
Our brilliant pins,

Stars in the late,
Black evening.

The Oak and the Grave

Père Lachaise Cemetery
Paris, France

Two hundred years it took the oak
To find the grave after its roots
Knuckled down to it in the yard.

Another hundred years,
A knotty elbow at the edge
Embraced it and the oak stretched

Its bony arms and leafy hands
Over a sea of stones, and took
Another century to lift

As if in praise the crypt from the dirt
Skew the lid, spill the fine
White dust from crevices

Carved by hand to signify
This final matter, claim it, expose
The faded etch of an ancient name.

I Heard the Word Ohio

O:

The beginning of a story:
An open, empty landscape
Without trees corn
Bending in the wind

Over the hill to the house.
A woman stops hoeing,
Resigns from the day, mops
Her brow with a huge kerchief

Under a fiery sky.
She sees a dust cloud down
The narrow road in the hills.
A friend is coming. O!

H:

A hinge upon a door.
The hasp that keeps the word
On earth. The O and I
Hang on its husky straps.

Helpless vowels, sticks
And circles. Without the H,
Like thumbs in her suspenders,
Any wind deep in the

Alveoli could make
Ohio a hale of letters.
Without the crossed roads
Of H, the driver is lost.

I:

Aspire. Look at light
Sky pins above
The highest hills dry
Of the Ohio river.

Wind flies in the corn
To make the sound of it
Echo in the valley.
It is her forearm brushing

Aside the stalks, crossing
Her brow to keep her sight
On the horizon clear.
Palm down, thumb back.

O:

Lovely is the word.
The breath of speaking it.
Almost a holy calling
On the open road.

Dust rises, distance
Closes between two women
Who, perhaps, had lost
Each other until now.

Song comes out the door.
Listen to the women
Sing it. Hear it closely:
O! I know why now I know.

Looking Out My Window, Three AM in Fremont

Electric moons oversee the trash
Ambling Thirty-fifth Street in the fitful

Wind off the lake. Chaos in the empty
Coffee house. Chairs overturned,

Alarmed in darkened windows
Face the cold remains of light.

The moon has its look. Geometry populates
The heavens of commerce

Lighted hills to the shore of the lake.
What is ventured

In the deep city, agreed upon
In the quiet darkness

The watchdogs sleeping at the gate?
What is the deal

When only stars are organized
And the incentive is the dark wind

Shredding legal clouds,
Hostile, taking over.

Snapshot at the Border

Southern Honduras, 1987

for KMR

Two happy campesinos. From behind
She throws one arm across his chest and says,
The words escaping from her silent mouth:
Let's stay. We can remain unnecessary,
Here like this in light and chemicals.
Embracing himself, he gazes out beyond
The boundary; the camera apprehends him.
The hardest part, she told us, was crossing there.
After this last trip, they found the tumor.
This shot could have been taken anywhere
But in Honduras, the sky blue as guns.
But that's where these two briefly made their protest.
Here she is holding her dying man,
Arrested, laughing, lips grazing his ear.

When Rick Died, Linda Said

She will toss his ashes in the Mekong,
The black grain an arc from her furrowed hand.
That seemed generous. When I am gone
My body will go to ruin in the land,
The soil in a garden comforting.
I will grow there, while my wife weeps
Above the decomposing birth of things.
I will lie in my ungenerous sleep.
I don't believe in spreading myself thin.
How would they ever find me? And who would try?
My travels done and every place I've been
Just punctuation in the dust when I die.
For myself, I need to find one place
With language carved in stone above my face.

Voyeur

I love a good night storm: shadows
Of tossed braches palm the walls
Of our house in the dark, search painted
Planes and cabinets with deft
Fingers to steal the names of lovers.

Carl Jung believed to dream of houses
Is to dream of the self. The human heart
Withheld in the framed home of the ribs
The flesh like windows that hold the storm
Away from the dry and lighted self.

I love to dream of splattered windows
Impervious to the fat rain pelts,
To choose to be within, or exit
And treat the rain as a confidante.
Standing here in the damp night

Rain on my head and down my neck
As if just surfaced from some depth
I watch the lighted squares like mirrors
Framed against the darkness, gestures
Of my neighbors moving room to room.

Crossing Agate Pass Bridge at Night

The lighted arms of the headlamps
Sweep the island's flats like forearms
Crossing a table. On the bridge,
Sky, land, and air become one darkness.

We signal with our hands in the shadows,
Talk as if we both had just emerged.
We wait for the next town to surface,
Tell us where we are, how far

To go, when we will arrive,
What lights to follow. We depend
On this frail current under the wheels.
You said you'd had a dream

The other night of falling in a car
Into a river, woke before the car could
Be swallowed in the Pass, algae lapped
At the door, silver tongues at the windows.

We will recognize arrival when
We see the running lights of Poulsbo,
And we break the surface of our
Small talk, startled, searching.

That little store with the dirt parking lot
And yellow neon sign, one letter
Blinking, lost, erratic,
Looks to me like an island in a night

That swallows light like a sea.
We hold our breath. We have come
So far our house is only a thought
That surfaces like other dreams

Fallen long ago into the river that
Find their way to the bank at last.
My wish is to remain here,
Suspended over the canal

In this dream, the shining arc,
Wheels spinning, until we waken
And emerge, breathless,
Silent as two islands.

The Eternal Interstate

The scrape of high-speed road noise.
Darkness screams like an animal.
Wool and steel in the welded seams,

High-pitched howls in the frame.
I'm an accident—I hear the plugs
Burn, the crankshaft crack and splinter,

The gear shift loosen, clutch pedal
Groan and clank, the floorboard buckle.
Screws unscrew and linger at my ear

Like tiny silver fairies who screech
And wag their magic wands in a new
And undone world—the windshield is

A symphony of tin—dying
I drift slowly in this ill-fit
Scratchy darkness, dog paddle

For a better view of the storm
On the eternal interstate—but maybe
Death is an opinion, a theory

A polite argument, a supposition
To explain the shattered glass.
But what a grand spectacle—

In my shirt of cosmic blue,
Buttons on fire, I watch the whole
Planet disengage with a click

And like a bald tire, bolts falling,
Twirl from the rim toward oblivion
The glittering debris, the burning stars.

Starlight Dome Car

Rain drools wind-blown on the Plexiglas.
The river angles once like the sleeve of a drowsy passenger.
Lumber bound in octagons and pentangles against the river.
The corrugated metal roof of the mill glows in muted light.
Out of moving trees, houses scatter like seagulls,

Little white-washed boxes, random as islands.
Under greasy clouds, a Chevy has run aground
Dismantled, then abandoned. It is an accident,
A heart's combustion decompressed. Rust runs in tributaries
From this piece of land children drive in wildly,

The miracle of play in a broken but still useful vehicle.
One incandescent bulb hangs lighted on an empty porch.
A kitchen wall, white as pumice, bathed in holy light,
Illuminates two penitents at the card table
Offering their kings and queens.

Code Blue

This summer evening
In the city,
A saxophonist
In an open window

Lets loose across the flat
Wire-crossed rooftops
His long, blue note
Like a siren.

At the hospital,
Code blue,
A different kind of
Music, the wheels

Of the crash cart
Drum the floor,
Instruments clink
As if they were

Tuning up
In the metal drawers.
Then, afterward,
At the end

Of pulmonary function,
The end of measure,
Telemetry
Switched off,

When she pushes the crash cart
Back down
The gleaming hallway
Slowly to its place,

It's like a pause,
A whole rest
Written into a kind of score,
Intentional,

The music in the silence
Between the notes.
But like music,
A new note always

Follows the interval:
Another patient,
The flourish
At change of shift,

What she carries
In the giant pockets
Of her scrubs—
Stethoscope,

Pen light to measure
Consciousness,
Dressings for the wounds
She can see—she braces

At the station,
Takes up the instrument
To call the family,
Finish—taking a breath—
The last note of the code.

Angiogram

The registration window of the hospital reminds me
Of crossing a border—documentation, destination,
Purpose—other entries into unseen territories.

In Bali, under the carved canopy draped with orchid vines,
The gaze of Goa Gaja that first morning, we sipped
Coffee, grainy and thick as the heat in windowless space.

Huge square windows in the hospital's long bright hallways,
Framed hydrangeas, rhododendrons, and clean refugees
Strolled in pale gowns, held onto IV poles like canes

And smiled to their visitors as those who have been rescued
To their rescuers. Heavy brown clouds of silt stirred
As I waded to my knees into the Indian Ocean

Warm as the morning in Bali. In Australia, flat beds
Jumbled into Perth, outlanders from oceans of dust.
Lorikeets blazed in mango trees. December in New Zealand

The President betrayed the Labor Party. We drove past
Cambridge, Maungatautari, maple colored sheep
In verdant fields to Coromandel, Northern Island,

And hot springs bubbled out of beach sand. My dense,
Unknown heart in the pale ocean of my body looks
Like Africa, the crooked finger of a river through it,

Tributaries like tiny bones, a solitary continent, a valve
That fluctuates like an eyelid to quake my sovereign heart.
When they inject the isotope, my heart radiates the heat of the sun.

Hypothermia

for Stephen and Daneen Kish

Rain drooled and swirled
In the mud lakes I trod through,
Fat rain drops thickly

Drenched three layers
Of sopping and drooping
Quick-dry synthetic.

Darkness infiltrated,
Stepped slowly through pine
Branches, like some being

Revealed as the one
Who will take over,
To whom the world yields

Without complaint,
Puts out its own lights.
I am extinguished

Here with the animals'
Dark and beautiful cries.

Neon Barista

She wears no clothes above Doc Martins,
Just tattoos. A uniform

Of neon epidermis: vines of roses
Twist at the branch of her elbow,

Waves of luminous green and blue
Evolve in circles from the smooth,

Round mountains of her breasts,
Concentric as the diagrams

Of earthquakes and tornadoes
Transfigure to the veins of plants,

And splotched ink dahlias bloom
From her hips; stars on her cheeks,

Her throat water, shoulders silver,
Forehead blue as a lake at the edge

Of the black forest of her dreadlocks.
She never need undress or dress.

Raking Leaves

The sound of all
This. Bamboo
Tines of the yard
Rake scrape

Stones. Rubber
Crunches on
The gravel. Wind
In the branches. Wind

Stirs the pile,
Leaves lift,
Dry, dead
Papery

To the sidewalk,
The street, the sweep
Of the rake in the pile,
Human breath.

Aubade

Sleepless again, 4 a.m.
I watch the backyard from behind

The cold glass of the bedroom window.
Leaves scattered and branches fell

In the night's wind. Limbs that remain
are poised to conduct the next gust,

And the glossy painted lawn chair waits
Like a seated gardener:

Thoughtful, contemplative, grateful
For the beginning and its bright dust.

Leaving Spain

We have come to the know meaning of departure.
The vowels rise, sown into the capes
Of toreros like the dust into the ring.
Flowers tossed from the stone seats.
The ancient ritual of human speech
Rises to the blue ceramic sky
Over the drought in the hills,
The white blood of the tiny cities.
Mosques, cathedrals, chapels.
The wine, the soil of Spain, the hills
Upon which lie the necklace of centuries.

The Third Door on the Left

I am now ten years older than my father was
When he died of a second heart attack.
Many of his brothers and their father had gone

Before, into the third door on the left down
The Hall of Everything that Came Before,
In suits, white shirts and thin black ties.

They uttered: *sacrifice, justice, peace.* Believed
Themselves worthy of the great turning
Of machines. Their keys jangled in their

Deep trouser pockets. They pointed out
The latest fixtures in the last bright passage
In which speech was possible.

Death is like an uncle: a man because I am a man.
He floats beside me, mirrors my whitening hair,
My purple veins, idle hands. How patient he is!

Could I say that death is optimistic? I hear him
Breathing softly—on a frosty morning
My breath clouds in front of me Tuesday or Saturday,

And a second set of fluffy white breath appears.
He is so polite I could introduce him as a colleague.
Many fathers, after their fried eggs and bacon

On white plates, had gone into the Third Door on the Left,
Into the last bright passage, and sketched in their open palms,
Their own last explanation. Approaching the threshold,

Still talking, they made room for each other,
Touched their snug collars, adjusted
To the light from the opening, the sudden illumination

That struck each one as they crossed into the lighted
Place. Then, as flexed fingers closed upon each heart,
They were stricken: *what tool made true a light this pure?*

Gunner Gets His Sea Legs

While I was seasick my first months
At sea, the boatswain's mate said:
S'all in ya haid, boa!
So I learned to right myself at sea:

When the starboard beam
Of the USS King slipped down, swollen
As a pot-bellied sailor, my dungarees
Flagged in the groaning gusts,

I remained upright starboard aft
In the hard turn, work boots
Black wedges flat on the non-skid
While the gray planet shifted rudder,

The wind veered and the splashing
Vessel sloped into the long turn.
I leaned into the curve of the earth
And put my face into the wind.

At the Coffee House

A man with a shaved head, maybe 50, sat in the red cloth chairs opposite a young woman, maybe 20 or 30, long dark hair clipped sloppily up at the back of her hooded sweatshirt, and listened to what seemed from the tone of her unsmiling talk, a serious life story—a man, I think—and I hear the word: "alcohol." Nothing else. I like to think he is her father. He listens. I like to think I know what he is thinking. What he doesn't say—

Look at you, he does not say. *You are so beautiful. You are miraculous, and by the inextricable knit that binds us I, too, am miraculous.*

His round face accommodates the soft, barely perceptible pleasure. But he realizes their existence here at this moment, being miraculous, that the miraculous is fragile, that the living of a thing implies its own demise, and this terrifies him. Behind them, the bright late spring morning glances off the window like a white hand. He looks distracted and glances about the room. He looks to contain his desperate yearning. He is on the brink, I know, of weeping only, falling to his knees, incoherent, despairing of comprehension, to be heard and released from his isolation at last—

How can you possibly understand, he begs at her feet. *How can you, young, beautiful daughter, grasp the brevity of the miraculous? The inevitability is more than I can bear!*

He buries his face in his hands. He takes a sip from the white paper cup. They get up to leave, staying just long enough for one latte each. They exit, passing through the light.

Biography

Gerry McFarland acquired his MFA in creative writing in 2011, served seven years on the editorial board of Floating Bridge Press, and taught psychology, human service and writing at the University of Phoenix until he retired to write full time. His poems have appeared in *Contemporary American Voices, Bayou, Crab Creek Review, Crucible, Limestone, Meridian Anthology of Contemporary Poetry, Sanscrit, Zyzzyva*, and the journal *War, Literature and the Arts*, among others. He was a finalist in the 2014 *december* Jeff Marks Memorial Poetry Prize, and his chapbook, *Gunner*, was a finalist in the Frost Place Chapbook Competition.